Table of Contents

The Scientific Method

The **scientific method** is the way scientists learn and study the world around them. You become a scientist when you try to find answers to your questions by using the scientific method.

Asking questions and coming up with answers is the basis for the scientific method. When you begin a science project, you begin with a question that you have. The educated guess you make about this question is called a **hypothesis**.

After you have asked the question and made an educated guess, you have to perform tests to determine whether or not your hypothesis is right. To test your hypothesis, you must follow a **procedure**, which is the name given to the steps you take in your experiment or fieldwork. Your experiment or fieldwork should give you information that can be measured. It is important to conduct your test multiple times and use as many test subjects as possible to make sure your results are consistent before you draw your conclusion.

Your **conclusion** describes how your **data**, or results you received from your experiment, compare to your hypothesis. A disproved hypothesis is just as important as a proven hypothesis because it gives important information to others. Your conclusion should also include any new questions that arise as you are doing your experiment.

Rumplestiltskin

Earth and Physical Science

 Sleuth Question: What are minerals and how do we identify them?

In the tale "Rumplestiltskin," a poor miller's daughter is forced to turn straw into gold. Of course, you know that this is not possible. Early chemists worked many hours to try to turn other metals into gold. To understand why it cannot work you need to know some things about minerals.

 Sleuth Notes

Gold is one of over 3,000 different minerals. A **mineral** is an inorganic, not living, crystal ingredient found in a rock. If you look at a rock closely, you can see the mineral crystals that hold it together. Think of a cookie as a rock. The ingredients that make a cookie are like the minerals that make a rock. Just as different ingredients make different kinds of cookies, different minerals form different kinds of rocks. There are about 6 basic ingredients that we use to make cookies. Yet we can make many different kinds. With over 3,000 different minerals, imagine how many different kinds of rocks nature can make!

 Sleuth Fact: Minerals are the nonliving crystal ingredients that form rock.

The minerals that make a rock occur naturally. This means that only nature can make a mineral. Minerals can be made in one of two ways. Cooling **magma** makes most minerals. Magma is nothing more than liquid rock. The inside of Earth acts as a huge oven, melting rock. When that magma begins to cool, the minerals crystallize and form new rocks. The type of rock made depends on the minerals it contains. Our Earth recycles itself. Old rocks get buried, melt, and then cool to form new rocks. The other way a mineral forms is called **precipitation**. In precipitation, minerals are formed as a mineral-containing solution, such as the ocean, evaporates. Salt is a common mineral formed this way.

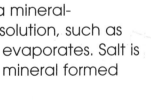  

 Sleuth Fact: Minerals are made by nature. They form from cooling magma or through precipitation.

Name: _____

Rumplestiltskin (cont.)

Minerals are always made with the same recipe and ingredients. Because each mineral has its own recipe, it also has its own properties. A **property** is a trait or characteristic that can be used to identify a substance. A cookie can be identified by the property of taste. There are many properties that can be used to identify a mineral. Some common ones include **color**, **hardness**, **streak color**, and **luster**. A mineral's hardness is found by testing what it scratches and what can scratch it. Some minerals, like a diamond, are very hard. Other minerals, like talc, are very soft. A mineral's hardness is ranked on a scale of 1–10. The hardest mineral, a diamond, has a hardness of ten. The softest mineral, talc, has a hardness of one. The color a mineral leaves behind when it is scratched on a streak plate tells its streak color. Gold leaves behind a yellow streak. Pyrite (fool's gold) has a greenish-brown streak. A mineral's luster tells the way it reflects light. Minerals that contain metal, like gold, are often shiny and have a metallic luster. Minerals that do not contain metal, like sulfur, may have a dull or greasy luster. Some minerals have special properties, such as being magnetic or glowing under a fluorescent light.

Sleuth Fact: Minerals can be identified through their properties.

Pre-Lab Questions

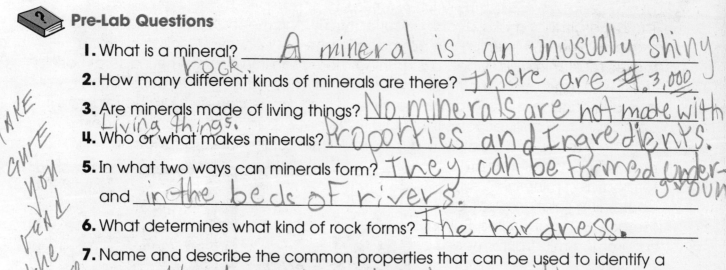

1. What is a mineral? _A mineral is an unusually shiny_ rock.

2. How many different kinds of minerals are there? _There are # 3,000_

3. Are minerals made of living things? _No minerals are not made with living things._

4. Who or what makes minerals? _Properties and Ingredients._

5. In what two ways can minerals form? _They can be Formed under-_ and _in the beds of rivers._ ground

6. What determines what kind of rock forms? _The hardness._

7. Name and describe the common properties that can be used to identify a mineral. _Hardness/ the streak/ magnitism/ metallic.lusters/ and biolumnhism._

_____

(handwritten margin note: MAKE SURE YOU READ the entire article)

Name: _____

Straw Into Gold (cont.)

Paper Clip Taken Out of Beaker After 20 Minutes

_____

Straw Taken Out of Beaker After 20 Minutes

_____

Pennies Taken Out of Vinegar and Salt

_____

Your Conclusions

What happened to the paper clip? _____

Why do you think this happened? _____

What happened to the straw? _____

Why do you think this happened? _____

Questions to Consider

I. Minerals can be made only from inorganic substances. What does this mean?

_____

2. Straw comes from a plant. Could straw be turned into a mineral, like gold? _____

Why? _____

3. Where do you think the copper color on your paper clip came from?_____

_____ Why? _____

Did the metal in your paper clip change into copper? _____ How do you

know? _____

4. Is there any possible way that Rumplestiltskin could have spun the king's straw into

gold? _____ Why or why not? _____

Name: _____

Are All Metals Magnetic?

This section of the workbook is called **physical science**. Physical science is the science of matter and energy and their interactions.

Starting Up

Are all metals equally magnetic? Try this simple test to see. Try to pick up a quarter with a magnet. Now, try a steel pin. Was there a difference?

Background

Most materials, even wood, copper, and water do not seem to respond to magnets. Although all materials can respond to magnetic force, some respond so weakly that the force is not observable. Items that respond well to magnets are iron, nickel, and cobalt.

Materials Needed

magnet
sharpened pencil (graphite)
straight pin (steel)
aluminum foil
copper wire
paper clip (steel)
penny (copper-plated zinc)
steel wool
nail (iron)
aluminum can
dime (copper and nickel)

Directions

Use the scientific method when conducting this and all experiments in this workbook. Test each of the items for its reaction to the magnet. Record your findings on the table on page 9.

Results

1. What types of metals are always magnetic?
2. What types of metals are not attracted to the magnet?

Applications and Extensions

Collect as many different metals as you can find. From what you have learned about different types of metals, predict which ones will be attracted to a magnet and which ones will not.

Why do mechanics sometimes magnetize their screwdrivers?

Name: _____

Are All Metals Magnetic?

List the items being tested in the table. Predict and then test each item against a magnet. Record whether each item is magnetic or nonmagnetic.

Item	Your Prediction	Is It Magnetic?	What Is It Made Of?

Research the items to determine their composition. Study the table.
What types of metals are always magnetic?

_____

What types of metals are never magnetic?

_____

Science Grade 5

Name: _____

Getting a Charge Out of It

Starting Up

⚠ What are negatively charged and positively charged materials and how are they different from each other? Spread some wax paper to use as a work surface. Sprinkle salt and pepper generously on the surface. Blow up a balloon and tie it. Hold it above, but not touching, the salt and pepper mixture. Observe what happens. Next, rub the balloon against your clothing for a few seconds. Again, hold it close to the mixture. What do you see?

Background

Atoms are made of negatively charged electrons orbiting a nucleus of positively charged protons and neutral neutrons. Some materials have a greater attraction for electrons than others do. They can "pull" electrons out of other material, creating a greater negative charge on their surfaces. In the demonstration, the balloon pulls electrons from your clothing. Because unlike charges attract, negatively charged material can attract positively charged material. This form of energy is known as **electrostatic energy**.

Materials Needed

a hard plastic ruler   a few stands pulled from a steel wool pad   newspaper
a piece of nylon stocking   l t. ground cinnamon

Directions

Spread a piece of newspaper to use as a work surface. Tear a small piece of newspaper in little pieces, about $\frac{1}{4}$ inch square, and place them in a pile. Make separate piles of the cinnamon and the steel wool strands. Rub the stocking along the ruler in one direction about 50 times. What happens when you bring the ruler near the top of the paper pile without touching it? Rub the ruler with the stocking again. This time place it near, but not touching, the top of the cinnamon pile. Next, put the ruler close to, but not touching, the steel wool.

Results

1. What did you observe? Is this similar to the pulls and pushes you observed when you experimented with magnets? (like poles repel and unlike poles attract)
2. Is something similar happening here though no magnetism is involved?

Applications and Extensions

Substitute one of the following materials for the plastic ruler: metal ruler, plastic cut from a milk carton, plastic or metal plate. Make another pile using one of the following materials: carpet samples, pieces of fake fur or wool, fine flour or powdered sugar, iron filings, Styrofoam packing pieces.

Research how lightning forms.

Name: _____

Getting a Charge Out of It

What is attracted to a negative charge?

Spread a piece of newspaper to use as a work surface. Put the items to be tested in small piles on the newspaper. Rub the stocking along the ruler about 50 times in one direction. Bring the ruler near the top of a pile without touching it. Draw and describe what you observe. Rub the stocking before approaching each pile.

Newspaper torn into little bits

_____
_____
_____
_____

A teaspoon of cinnamon

_____
_____
_____
_____

Steel wool strands

_____
_____
_____
_____

Label each of the following diagrams as POSSIBLE or IMPOSSIBLE. Explain why.

A. _____   **A.** _____
_____
_____
_____

B. _____   **B.** _____
_____
_____
_____

Far and Little, Close and Big

Starting Up

Have an adult pound several nails part way into a block of wood. Have him or her show you how to use the claw of a hammer to remove a nail. Then, try removing the nails while you observe all the points where force is applied. Try holding the handle close to the fulcrum and far from the fulcrum. Which works better?

Background

Think of a teeter-totter. A person who is light should sit at the far end. A heavier person should sit closer to the middle, or fulcrum. This balances the load and allows the teeter-totter to move back and forth easily.

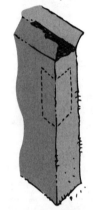

Materials Needed

10 pennies
modeling clay
a cereal box
ruler
scissors

Directions

Cut part of a folded edge of a cereal box (as pictured). Secure the folded cardboard to a desk with clay. This becomes the fulcrum for the ruler. Center the ruler on the fulcrum and balance five pennies on both ends. Then put six pennies on one side and four on the other. Experiment with moving the ruler on the fulcrum to balance or move the pennies up and down the ruler. Try other penny combinations and attempt to come up with a general explanation for how to balance a load by changing the length of the lever or the placement of the load.

Results

What did you discover?

Applications and Extensions

The long-handled hammers in a piano magnify the force applied by the pianist's fingers. How does a teeter-totter work?

Name: _____

Far and Little, Close and Big

How can you balance different loads?

Predict whether each setup will balance. Draw an equal sign (=) over the drawings that you think will balance. If you think a ruler will tip, add an arrow to show which direction. Build each setup with your ruler, fulcrum, and pennies. Check your predictions and write a sentence explaining the results.

I.
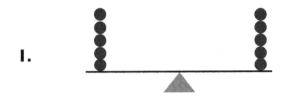

_____

_____

2.

_____

_____

3.
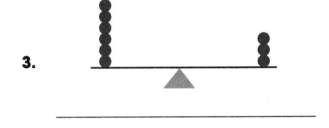

_____

_____

4.
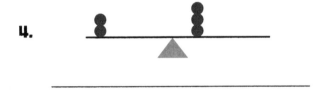

_____

_____

5.
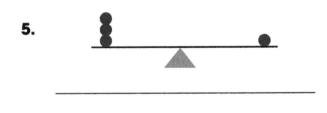

_____

_____

6.
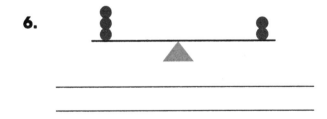

_____

_____

Draw other balanced arrangements you tried.

_____   _____

_____   _____

What did you discover about balancing loads with a lever and fulcrum?

_____

_____

Black and White Light

Starting Up

⚠ Put a lightbulb in a gooseneck lamp. Without touching either the lamp or the bulb, which can burn, move your hands under the lighted bulb and feel the heat. What do you know about heat and light? Are these forms of energy the same? Do they always go together?

Background

Visible light is made up of a range of wavelengths from the comparatively short waves near the ultraviolet to the longer waves near the infrared. Infrared rays are hot and create heat. A black light emits shorter waves closer to the ultraviolet range and creates less heat. Full spectrum light emits longer wavelengths, and therefore, more heat.

Materials Needed

two gooseneck lamps
two sheets of white paper
two thermometers or
    aquarium temperature strips
a 60-watt black lightbulb
a 60-watt transparent-glass lightbulb
a ruler

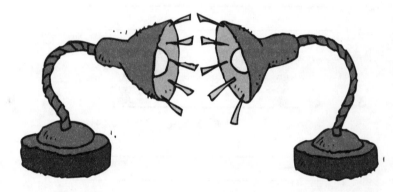

Directions

Place the lightbulbs in the two lamps, but do not turn on the lamps yet. Put the lamps on a large table about two feet apart. Place the thermometers or temperature strips on the sheets of paper under the lamps equidistant from the bulbs (about 8 inches apart). Record the temperature of both thermometers on a chart. Turn on the lamps. Record the temperatures on your chart every 5 minutes for the next hour.

Results

Record the data from your chart onto the double line graph on page 15. What were your results?

Applications and Extensions

Repeat the experiment, but change the height of the lightbulbs or the color of the paper. Compare your results.

What color lightbulbs do pet shops use to keep lizards and snakes warm at night? Why does this work?

Name: _____

Black and White Light

How are lights different?

Make a double-line graph to plot your data. Write the temperature increments on the left axis. Create a key to explain the different lines or colors representing the different bulbs.

How Do Different Bulbs Heat?

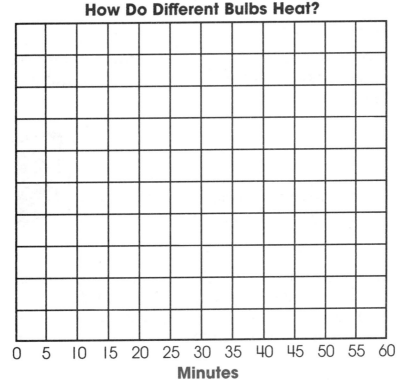

0 5 10 15 20 25 30 35 40 45 50 55 60
Minutes

Key
Black light
White light

Which bulb created more heat? Explain.

_____

_____

Look at the table of the electromagnetic spectrum. Why does a white lightbulb produce more heat than a black lightbulb?

_____

_____

_____

_____

_____

The Electromagnetic Spectrum

HOT

radio waves

infrared
visible light   ROY G. BIV
ultraviolet
x-rays

gamma rays   COLD

Name: _____

Now You See It, Now You Don't

Starting Up
Wind up a toy and let it move across the table or floor until it stops. Why did it move and why did it stop? Energy is neither created nor destroyed. It is only changed in form. Where did the energy for the movement come from?

Background
Kinetic energy is the energy of movement. Kinetic energy may be stored as **potential energy**, which can be released at a later time. As energy changes from potential to kinetic, some is lost as heat.

Materials Needed
two sizes of plastic bags
a variety of school supplies (different weights)

Directions
Put an object that weighs about a half pound (like a crayon box) in the larger plastic bag. Hold the top of the bag with one hand and twist the bag five times with the other hand. What happens when you release the hand that was twisting the bag? Repeat this experiment using the smaller bag and compare your results. Test bag sizes and masses. What combination of mass and bag size causes the bag to turn back on itself and spin in the opposite direction?

Results
How is the bag like the wind-up toy? What is the original source of energy? Why do the bags and the toy eventually stop moving? Where do you think the energy goes?

Applications and Extensions
Make predictions and test your hypotheses about other variables, such as the number of twists given to the bag.

Research and find out: How do wind-up clocks work? How does a bicycle use stored energy?

Name: _____

Now You See It, Now You Don't

How can energy be stored?

Draw a picture of the larger bag with the half-pound object in it. Twist the bag exactly five times and release. Describe what happens.

_____

_____

_____

Put the half-pound object in the smaller bag. Twist the bag exactly five times and release. Describe what happens. Compare the results to the first trial.

_____

_____

_____

Put a different object in the first bag. Draw a picture of the bag. Twist the bag exactly five times and release. Describe what happens. Compare the results to the other trials.

_____

_____

_____

Try another variable.

_____ (record variable)

Twist the bag and release. Describe what happens. Compare the results to the other trials.

_____

_____

Label each picture as *kinetic* or *potential* energy.

_____   _____

Name: _____

Moving Through a Membrane

This section of the workbook is called **life science**. Life science is any of the branches of natural science dealing with the structure and behavior of living organisms.

Starting Up
How many cells does a chicken egg have?

Materials Needed
2 eggs	vinegar	salt
water	3 small bowls	corn syrup

Background
The common chicken egg is actually one cell. The largest single cell is the egg of the ostrich. While expensive, they can be obtained from farms that raise ostriches. The shell of an egg is a protective layer of calcium carbonate that is deposited around the cell membrane. This activity uses the selectivity of the cell membrane to allow water to pass back and forth, but the shell must first be removed. The activity, then, is in two parts. The first part is the process to remove the calcium carbonate by dissolving the shell in vinegar, and the second step shows **osmosis**, or the passage or diffusion, of a material through a semipermeable membrane (the inner membrane of the chicken egg).

Procedure

Dissolving the Eggshell
1. Record how a chicken egg feels when holding it. Describe the shell.
2. Carefully place two eggs, without cracks, into a small bowl. Cover them completely with vinegar.
3. Keep the eggs in the vinegar for 24 hours.
4. Rinse the eggs after the shells have been removed in clean water. Describe how the eggs feel and look.

Applications and Extensions
Social Studies
• Write about countries in which pure drinking water is not as plentiful as it is in the United States and about the processes they use to obtain freshwater.

Mathematics
• Weigh each of the eggs before and after the experiment to calculate the percentage change in the weight of the egg caused by the movement of water.

Eggs Not Soaked in Vinegar	Eggs Soaked in Vinegar

Observing Osmosis

1. Fill two bowls about two-thirds full with water.
2. Stir 2 tablespoons of salt into one bowl of water.
3. Add $\frac{1}{2}$ cup of corn syrup to the other bowl.
4. Place one rinsed egg in each bowl.
5. Observe what happens to the eggs during the next 12—24 hours. How does each egg look now? Draw each egg to show what has happened.

Sugar Water	Salt Water

Questions

1. The egg is surrounded by a membrane without any smaller divisions. What is the term that describes this unit building block of life? _____

2. Which egg became larger? smaller? _____

3. Which egg shows that material can move *into* a cell?_____

4. Which egg shows that material can move *out* of a cell?_____

5. If you put your hand in salt water, what will happen to the cells of your hand? _____
   _____

6. Why is your hand "shriveled up" after you come out of the ocean or swimming pool?
   _____

7. What would happen to the cells in your body if you drank salt water?_____
   _____

8. Why is freshwater important to cells in your body?_____
   _____

Name: _____

Life in the Soil

Starting Up
What lives in the soil?

Materials Needed
newspaper
small garden shovel
large bucket
magnifying glass
bug magnifier box
apron or old shirt
large resealable plastic bag
small piece of leather (from old shoe or purse)
water
soil

Setup
 Collect the soil in large buckets without disturbing too much of the surrounding areas.

Procedure
Select an area that has rich soil where invertebrates are living. Good options include wooded areas where you can clear away leaves or carefully move decaying logs. It is important to collect the soil just before you need to use it so the soil does not dry out. For the second half of the activity, mold and mildew comes from the soil and piece of leather; plants sprout from seeds trapped in the soil; and, possibly, insects will hatch from eggs buried in the soil. Make your observations on days one, two, four, five, seven, and eight. Fill in your observations on the data sheet found on page 23.

Name: _____

Applications and Extensions
Science
• Visit a greenhouse and find out how unwanted seeds and microbes in the soil are avoided.
• Place some soil on a petri dish with the nutrient agar to observe soil nematodes tunneling through the agar.

Math
• Create a pie chart depicting the different things that are growing in your miniature environment.

Language Arts
• Write a short story about living in the soil from the viewpoint of one of the creatures you observed.

Social Studies
• Research third world countries to find out what difficulties the people may have in growing types of plants from seeds. Compare and contrast their types of soil to yours.

Name: _____

Life in the Soil

Procedure

1. Observe anything that is crawling around on top trying to bury itself back in the soil. Carefully place them in bug magnifier boxes and examine them. Make observations.
2. Carefully push the soil sideways to spread it out evenly on newspaper. Make observations and record them on a sheet of paper.
3. Pick up a handful of the soil and examine it closely using the magnifying glass.
4. Take some new soil (not the soil you just examined) and pour it into a resealable plastic bag.
5. Place a small piece of used leather in the bag, then sprinkle the soil and leather with water.
6. Seal the plastic bag, making sure to trap air in the upper part of the bag. Set the bag in a sunny location.
7. Check the bag on days 1, 2, 4, 5, 7, and 8. Watch for new plants or animals growing in the bag. Mold, mildew, seedlings, grasses, and small insects that were trapped in the soil may possibly emerge. Record your observations on your data sheet.

Questions
Observing the Soil

1. What types of invertebrates do you see living in the soil? _____

    _____

2. Draw two of the invertebrates you observed. Include in the pictures details about the environment and what the animals were doing.

Miniature Environment

3. Describe and draw pictures of the miniature environment each day.
4. From where do you think the new life came? _____

    _____

Name: _____

Life in the Soil Data Sheet

Day 1	Day 2	Day 4

Day 5	Day 7	Day 8

Name: _____

Observing the Life Cycle of a Butterfly

Starting Up
Can you name the different life cycles of
a butterfly?

Materials Needed
butterfly house
butterfly eggs
food for caterpillars/butterflies
pictures of the stages of the butterfly life cycle
journal
markers and pencil

Introduction
The caterpillar hatches from an egg as a tiny **larva**, feeds, and grows until it is time to
form the **chrysalis**, then finally emerges as a butterfly. This is called a **complete
metamorphosis**. In this activity, you will make daily observations of caterpillars to
understand the life cycle of a butterfly.

Procedure
  1. Observe the area each day and record your observations on your data sheet.
  2. You may wish to keep a journal as well.
  3. Carefully monitor the climate and food supply for the insects. Butterfly eggs and a
     butterfly house can be ordered from a science supply catalog. Special instructions
     are included with the order. It is important to complete the activity at the proper
     time of the year so the butterflies can be released outdoors.

Applications and Extensions
Science
• Explore other insects' life cycles to find out about incomplete metamorphosis and
  complete metamorphosis.
• Raise crickets and mealworms and observe their life cycles.

Name: _____

Observing the Life Cycle of a Butterfly Data Sheet

Day _____

Day _____

Day _____

Day _____

Day _____

Day _____

Name: _____

The Shape of a Bird's Beak

Starting Up
Have you ever noticed how different birds' beaks are shaped? The shape of a bird's beak helps the bird obtain the food it eats. Birds' beaks are specially adapted.

Materials Needed

pliers or tweezers	beads
straws	soda bottle
coffee stirrers	cotton balls
kitchen spoons	small plastic fish
clothespins	pictures of various birds
egg carton	shallow pan

Introduction
The shape of a bird's beak serves a very important purpose in its survival. Different birds have differently shaped beaks. The hummingbird has a very thin beak resembling a straw which allows it to sip the nectar from a bell-shaped flower; the cardinal's triangular-shaped beak is used to break open the shells of various seeds; and the pelican's large scoop-shaped beak allows it to catch fish. In this activity, you will have the opportunity to experiment with different "beak shapes" to find out how this adaptation helps each bird to survive.

Procedure
1. Look in an encyclopedia or bird book for pictures of a few birds with differently shaped beaks.
2. How does the shape of each beak affect the kind of food it eats?
3. Birds have beaks in certain shapes to assist them in obtaining food. The shape of the beak is a special adaptation.
4. Place the following items into a shallow pan:
   • beads to represent seeds such as sunflowers
   • cotton balls to represent different types of berries
   • small plastic fish to represent aquatic life forms
   • the egg carton with beads in it to represent a tree with insects
   • a soda bottle to represent the opening of a flower
5. Find out which type of beak is best suited for obtaining certain foods.
6. See the lab sheet on page 28 for further instructions.

Name: _____

Applications and Extensions
Mathematics
• Create a graph that represents trials versus successful captures of food for each of the types of bird beaks and each type of food.

Science
• Describe how a bird of prey's beak looks. This type of bird has a very sharp beak for tearing apart its food.
• Investigate the different types of birds of prey and what they eat.

Language Arts
• Write a story or poem from the perspective of the bird who is trying to catch its food. An example might be a woodpecker who is pecking away on a tree in search of insects.

Art
• Create a diorama of a bird actually searching for its food. Make sure the food and beak type are correct.

Name: _____

The Shape of a Bird's Beak

Procedure

1. Investigate to find out which "beak" is the best choice for picking up each "food" in the pan. Kinds of "beaks" provided:
   - pliers or tweezers for a long, narrow beak
   - clothespin for a triangular or squared-off beak
   - spoon for a larger beak that is able to scoop up food
   - straw or coffee stirrer for a thin, narrow beak
2. Do not use your hands to hold anything except the "beak." Carefully touch the surrounding parts of the food such as the egg carton and soda bottle with the "beak."
3. Tell how you collected each type of food.

Food	"Beak" Used
beads (seeds)	
cotton balls (berries)	
plastic fish	
egg carton (tree with insects in bark)	
soda bottle (trumpet-shaped flowers)	

4. Draw the different types of beaks below.

Name a bird that has a beak like this:

_____   _____   _____   _____

Kinds of food eaten by each type of bird:

_____   _____   _____   _____

Questions

1. Why is it important that birds have differently shaped beaks? _____
   _____

2. Describe a type of bird you see in your area. What kind of beak does that bird have? What foods does it eat?_____
   _____

3. How is the shape of a bird's beak a special adaptation? _____
   _____

Make Your Own Volcano

This section of the workbook is called **earth science**. Earth science is any of the sciences dealing with earth and its parts, including outer space.

Materials Needed
vinegar, red food coloring, a large cardboard box, baking soda, a narrow plastic beaker, sand, a paper towel tube, scissors, clay, a flat box (3-4" high), an X-acto™ knife, masking tape

⚠️ Cut and tape a flat box together so that it is about 10" square. Color the vinegar with red food coloring. Wear old clothes for the eruption. Make sure an adult is present during the experiment.

Directions

1. Fill half of a beaker with baking soda.

2. Cut two or three holes in the paper towel tube. Put it over the beaker.

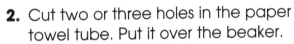

3. Mold clay around the tube. Leave the top and the holes you poked open.

4. Make tunnels out of clay that lead down to the holes.

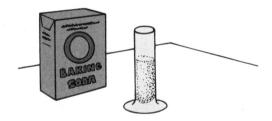

5. Put the beaker with the tube molded with clay in the large box. Pile damp sand around the clay volcano. Pat it to make it into a volcano shape. Leave the top and tunnels exposed.

6. When it is time to make it erupt, take it outside. Pour red vinegar into the beaker. Stand back. **VOOM!**

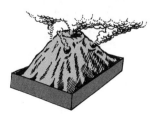

Name: _____

Continental Puzzle

Starting Up
Look at the map below of the supercontinent Pangea. Why does the map not now fit together with 100% accuracy?

Materials Needed
map of the continents (page 32)
sheet of thin or tracing paper
construction paper
school glue
scissors
large map of the world

Procedure
See instructions on page 31.

Applications and Extensions
Mathematics
• Determine by ratios size comparisons of the continents.
• Estimate the accuracy of fit by estimating the area of the supercontinent assembled and estimating the area of overlap and gaps using graph paper for the continents.

Science
• Compare fossil remains on edges of continental plates and draw conclusions.

Language Arts
• Write a report regarding the evidence for or against Pangea.

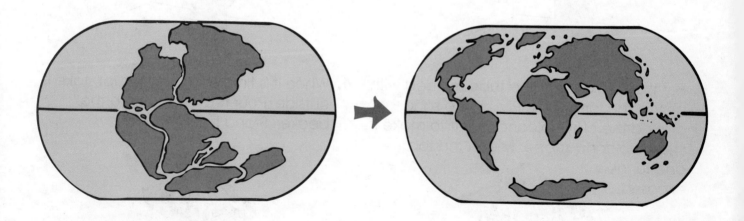

Name: _____

Continental Puzzle

Procedure

1. Trace and cut out the continents map on page 32.
2. Place the continent shapes on a piece of paper in the arrangement they now have on the globe's surface. If needed, refer to the world map.
3. Millions of years ago, the continents formed one supercontinent called *Pangea*. Since that time the continents have moved to their present positions following the breakup of Pangea. Reverse this process and try to fit the continents together as one huge continent.
4. Do not move the continents through or across each other. They may be moved in straight lines, rotated, or in large arcs.
5. When you find what you believe is the "best fit," glue the pieces in place on a dark piece of construction paper.

Questions

1. Do the continents fit exactly together? _____

   _____

   _____

2. Do you have places where the continents overlap? What may cause this overlap?

   _____

   _____

3. Do you have places where the continents have gaps between them? What may cause these gaps? _____

   _____

   _____

Name: _____

Continental Map Pattern

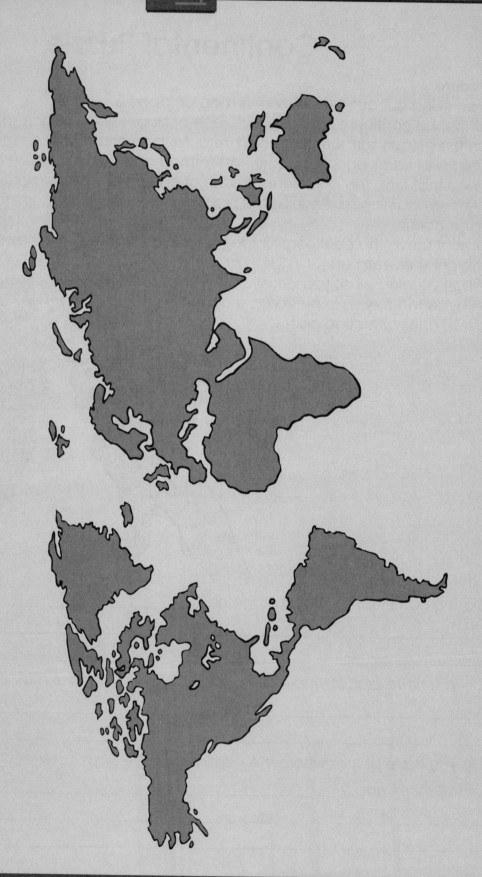

Name: _____

Physical Characteristics of the Planets

Starting Up
Does it take longer for an outer planet to orbit the Sun than it does for an inner planet to orbit the Sun? Why?

Materials Needed
playground area   string
sidewalk chalk   stopwatch
measuring tape

Introduction
Each planet in our solar system has unique characteristics. For example, Saturn is well known for having a massive set of rings made of ice and debris. However, did you also know that Jupiter and Uranus have a series of rings? This activity will explain one major characteristic of the planets and allow for the exploration of the others through books.

Preparation
1. Using the chart provided, develop a scale version of the distance from the Sun for each planet. A scale version is provided for you, but you also may develop your own.
2. Select a point for the Sun somewhere in the center of the playground. Using sidewalk chalk, draw a picture of the Sun.
3. Using the scale version of the distance from the Sun to Mercury, measure the distance and draw Mercury.
4. Draw a partial orbit for Mercury around the Sun. A good way of constructing an arc for the partial orbit is to stand in the center of the Sun with a long piece of string which reaches to Mercury. Have someone else hold that string and, using the chalk, draw the arc for the partial orbit around the Sun.
5. Continue the process of measuring a planet's distance from the Sun and then drawing a partial arc for its orbit, until each planet is represented.
6. Follow Step 4 for making each arc. By doing this, each orbit will be as circular as possible, although planets' orbits are really elliptical.

Procedure
1. After your solar system is complete, begin with the orbit of Mercury and walk along the orbit for one minute by placing one foot directly in front of the other in a toe to heel fashion.
2. How far do you have to move to complete an orbit around the Sun?
3. Repeat steps 1 and 2 with each planet's orbit.

Applications and Extensions
Math
• Develop different scale distances for the planets and redo this activity.
• Look up how many days it takes each planet to orbit the Sun to determine its "year." Figure out how old you would be on each planet. Would you be older or younger than you are now on each planet?
• Continue this activity in a very large area and determine how many steps it would take to actually orbit the "Sun" as a particular planet and the time required. Compare those numbers to actual data.

Language Arts
• Write riddles or puzzles about the planets based on factual information. Have a family member try to solve these riddles.
• Write a Haiku about each planet, describing the conditions on the planet, the planet's weather, or other nature-related items.

Art
• Using a smaller scale, design and draw a mural of the solar system. Paint identifiable characteristics on each planet.

Social Studies
• Read about the planets and identify in which age each was discovered. For example, the inner planets were known during the time of the Ancients and were referred to as the "wanderers."

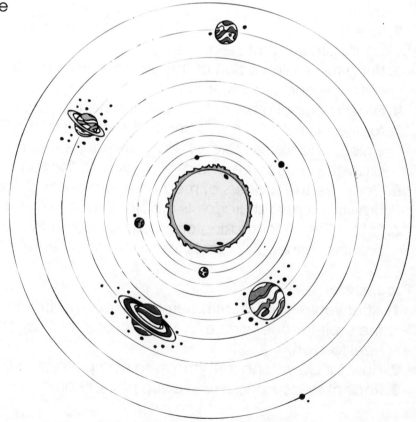

Name: _____

Physical Characteristics of the Planets

Procedure

How far around the Sun can you walk in one minute in each planet's orbit? Compare the distances.

Planet	Average Distance to Sun (Millions of Kilometers)	Scale Distance (Meters)	Your Scale Distance
Mercury	58	.55	
Venus	108	1.02	
Earth	150	1.42	
Mars	228	2.17	
Jupiter	778	7.37	
Saturn	1429	13.51	
Uranus	2875	27.30	
Neptune	4504	42.61	
Pluto	5900	55.91	

Questions

1. What did you notice about the distances of the inner planets from the Sun compared to the outer planets' distances from the Sun? _____

_____

2. Describe what happened to the distance you traveled around the Sun on each planet's orbit as you got further away from the Sun. _____

_____

3. Why do you think it takes a longer period of time for Pluto and Neptune to travel around the Sun than it does for Mercury? _____

_____

4. If it takes longer for the outer planets to travel around the Sun, what happened to the length of each planet's year? Explain your answer. _____

_____

Science Grade 5

Name: _____

Space Snowballs

Planets and moons are not the only objects in our solar system that travel in orbits. Comets also orbit the Sun.

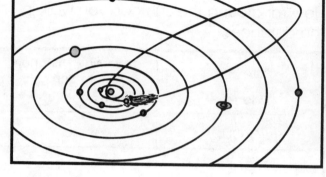

A **comet** is like a giant dirty snowball that is $\frac{1}{2}$ to 3 miles wide. It is made of frozen gases, dust, ice, and rocks.

As the comet gets closer to the Sun, the frozen gases melt and evaporate. Dust particles float in the air. The dust forms a cloud called a **coma**. The "wind" from the Sun blows the coma away from the Sun. The blowing coma forms the comet's tail.

There are more than 800 known comets. Halley's Comet is the most famous. It appears about every 76 years. The last scheduled appearance in this century was in 1985. When will it appear next?

Find the words from the Word Bank in the word search. When you are finished, write down the letters that are not circled. Start at the top of the puzzle and go from left to right.

Word Bank

dust	orbit
Halley	tail
coma	ice
snowball	sky
melt	shining
solar system	

```
S P M E L T L A N H E
O T S S H A C O M A V
L E N O R D B I T L S
A L O I K U E C I L R
R C W L E S S C O E M
S E B T S T H A V Y E
Y O A R O R B I T B I
S T L S S H A P E D L
T I L K T A I L E A F
E O O T I C E B A L L
M S K Y S H I N I N G
```

_ _ _ _ _ _ _ _ _ _ _ _ _ _ _ _ _ _ _

_ _ _ _ _ _ _ . _ _ _ _ _ _ _ _ _ _ _ _ _ _ _ _

_ _ _ _ _ _ _ _ _ _ _ _ _ _ _ _ _ _ _ _ _ .

---

page 4

SCIENTIFIC INQUIRY Name: _____

Rumplestiltskin (cont.)

Minerals are always made with the same recipe and ingredients. Because each mineral has its own recipe, it also has its own properties. A **property** is a trait or characteristic that can be used to identify a substance. A cookie can be identified by the property of taste. There are many properties that can be used to identify a mineral. Some common ones include **color, hardness, streak color,** and **luster.** A mineral's hardness is found by testing what it scratches and what can scratch it. Some minerals, like a diamond, are very hard. Other minerals, like talc, are very soft. A mineral's hardness is ranked on a scale of 1-10. The hardest mineral, a diamond, has a hardness of ten. The softest mineral, talc, has a hardness of one. The color a mineral leaves behind when it is scratched on a streak plate tells its streak color. Gold leaves behind a yellow streak. Pyrite (fool's gold) has a greenish-brown streak. A mineral's luster tells the way it reflects light. Minerals that contain metal, like gold, are often shiny and have a metallic luster. Minerals that do not contain metal, like sulfur, may have a dull or greasy luster. Some minerals have special properties, such as being magnetic or glowing under a fluorescent light.

Sleuth Fact: Minerals can be identified through their properties.

Pre-Lab Questions

1. a naturally occurring inorganic solid crystal found in rocks
2. over 3,000
3. Minerals are made only of inorganic, not living things.
4. nature
5. cooling magma and precipitation
6. the types of minerals it contains
7. luster—the way a mineral reflects light
   streak color—the color a mineral marks on a streak plate
   hardness—what a mineral can scratch and what scratches the mineral

Science Grade 5   4

---

page 6

SCIENTIFIC INQUIRY Name: _____

Straw Into Gold (cont.)

Sleuth Question: Can straw be turned into a metal like gold?

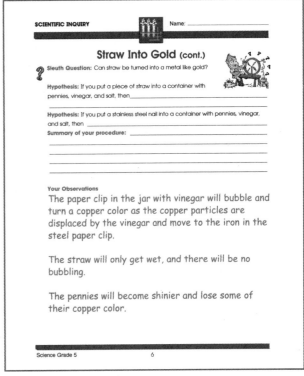

Hypothesis: If you put a piece of straw into a container with pennies, vinegar, and salt, then _____

Hypothesis: If you put a stainless steel nail into a container with pennies, vinegar, and salt, then _____
Summary of your procedure: _____
_____
_____
_____
_____

Your Observations

The paper clip in the jar with vinegar will bubble and turn a copper color as the copper particles are displaced by the vinegar and move to the iron in the steel paper clip.

The straw will only get wet, and there will be no bubbling.

The pennies will become shinier and lose some of their copper color.

Science Grade 5   6

---

page 7

SCIENTIFIC INQUIRY Name: _____

Straw Into Gold (cont.)

Paper Clip Taken Out of Beaker After 20 Minutes

Straw Taken Out of Beaker After 20 Minutes

Pennies Taken Out of Vinegar and Salt

Your Conclusions

What happened to the paper clip? The paper clip got a copper coating on the part that was in the solution.

Why do you think this happened? _____

What happened to the straw? The straw softened.

Why do you think this happened? _____

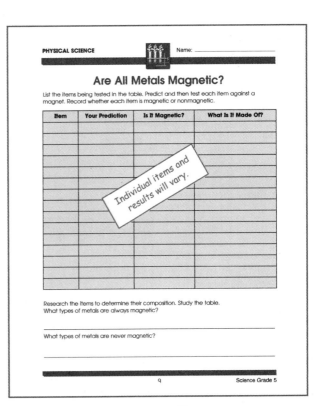

Questions to Consider

1. Inorganic means that a substance has never been living.
2. No, straw comes from living things; minerals can be made only of things that have never been living.
3. Answers will vary.
4. No, only nature can make a mineral.

7   Science Grade 5

---

page 9

PHYSICAL SCIENCE Name: _____

Are All Metals Magnetic?

List the items being tested in the table. Predict and then test each item against a magnet. Record whether each item is magnetic or nonmagnetic.

Item	Your Prediction	Is It Magnetic?	What Is It Made Of?

Individual items and results will vary.

Research the items to determine their composition. Study the table.
What types of metals are always magnetic?

_____

What types of metals are never magnetic?

_____

9   Science Grade 5

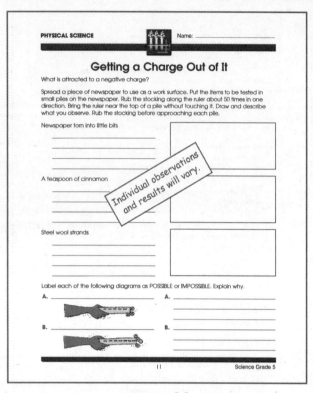

page 11

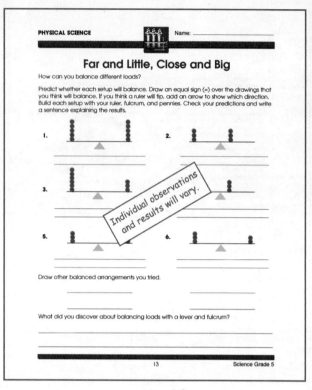

page 13

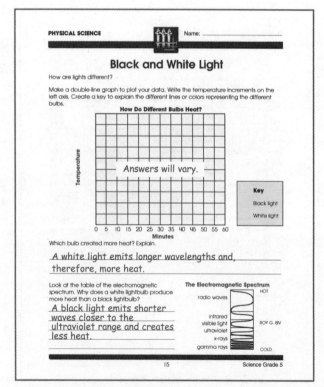

page 15

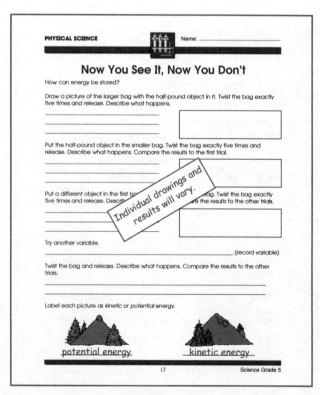

page 17

page 19

Eggs Not Soaked in Vinegar	Eggs Soaked in Vinegar

Observing Osmosis
1. Fill two bowls about two-thirds full with water.
2. Stir 2 tablespoons of salt into one bowl of water.
3. Add ¼ cup of corn syrup to the other bowl.
4. Place one rinsed egg in each bowl.
5. Observe what happens to the eggs during the next 12–24 hours. How does each egg look now? Draw each egg to show what has happened.

Sugar Water	Salt Water

Questions
1. Cell
2. The egg in sugar water became larger than the other egg. The egg in salt water was smaller.
3. The egg in sugar water absorbed water and changed in size.
4. The egg in salt water shrunk in size because water left the egg.
5. They will shrink and shrivel if left in the water for a long enough period of time.
6. There are salts found in both the pool and the oceans which cause water to move out of the cells in your hand.
7. They would shrink in size because water would leave the cells.
8. Freshwater is important for moving water into cells and replacing existing water that may have salts in it.

19   Science Grade 5

page 22

Life in the Soil

Procedure
1. Observe anything that is crawling around on top trying to bury itself back in the soil. Carefully place them in bug magnifier boxes and examine them. Make observations.
2. Carefully push the soil sideways to spread it out evenly on newspaper. Make observations and record them on a sheet of paper.
3. Pick up a handful of the soil and examine it closely using the magnifying glass.
4. Take some new soil (not the soil you just examined) and pour it into a resealable plastic bag.
5. Place a small piece of used leather in the bag, then sprinkle the soil and leather with water.
6. Seal the plastic bag, making sure to trap air in the upper part of the bag. Set the bag in a sunny location.
7. Check the bag on days 1, 2, 4, 5, 7, and 8. Watch for new plants or animals growing in the bag. Mold, mildew, seedlings, grasses, and small insects that were trapped in the soil may possibly emerge. Record your observations on your data sheet.

Questions
1. Answers will vary.
2. Answers will vary.
3. Answers will vary.
4. Answers will vary. For example, mold and mildew may have come from the soil or have been located on the leather; seeds could have been trapped in the soil; and insect eggs may be buried in the soil.

Science Grade 5   22

page 25

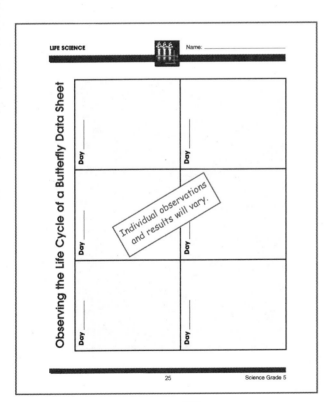

Observing the Life Cycle of a Butterfly Data Sheet

Individual observations and results will vary.

25   Science Grade 5

page 28

The Shape of a Bird's Beak

Procedure
1. Investigate to find out which "beak" is the best choice for picking up each "food" in the pan. Kinds of "beaks" provided:
   - pliers or tweezers for a long, narrow beak
   - clothespin for a triangular or squared-off beak
   - spoon for a larger beak that is able to scoop up food
   - straw or coffee stirrer for a thin, narrow beak
2. Do not use your hands to hold anything except the "beak." Carefully touch the surrounding parts of the food such as the egg carton and soda bottle with the "beak."
3. Tell how you collected each type of food.

Food	"Beak" Used
beads (seeds)	
cotton balls (berries)	
plastic fish	
egg carton (tree with insects in bark)	
soda bottle (trumpet-shaped flowers)	

4. Draw the different types of beaks below.

Name a bird that has a beak like this: _____

Kinds of food eaten by each type of bird: _____

Questions
1. Answers will vary. For example, each bird is able to get the type of food it needs to survive.
2. Answers will vary.
3. The beak enables the bird to feed on specific foods.

Science Grade 5   28

ANSWER KEY

EARTH SCIENCE

Name: _____

Continental Puzzle

Procedure
1. Trace and cut out the continents map on page 32.
2. Place the continent shapes on a piece of paper in the arrangement they now have on the globe's surface. If needed, refer to the world map.
3. Millions of years ago, the continents formed one supercontinent called *Pangea.* Since that time the continents have moved to their present positions following the breakup of Pangea. Reverse this process and try to fit the continents together as one huge continent.
4. Do not move the continents through or across each other. They may be moved in straight lines, rotated, or in large arcs.
5. When you find what you believe is the "best fit," glue the pieces in place on a dark piece of construction paper.

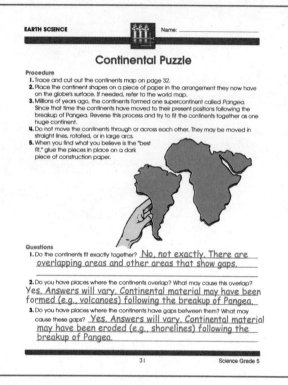

Questions
1. Do the continents fit exactly together? <u>No, not exactly. There are overlapping areas and other areas that show gaps.</u>

2. Do you have places where the continents overlap? What may cause this overlap? <u>Yes. Answers will vary. Continental material may have been formed (e.g., volcanoes) following the breakup of Pangea.</u>

3. Do you have places where the continents have gaps between them? What may cause these gaps? <u>Yes. Answers will vary. Continental material may have been eroded (e.g., shorelines) following the breakup of Pangea.</u>

31   Science Grade 5

page 31

EARTH SCIENCE

Name: _____

Physical Characteristics of the Planets

Procedure
How far around the Sun can you walk in one minute in each planet's orbit? Compare the distances.

Planet	Average Distance to Sun (Millions of Kilometers)	Scale Distance (Meters)	Your Scale Distance
Mercury	58	.55	
Venus	108	1.02	
Earth	150	1.42	
Mars	228	2.17	
Jupiter	778	7 .37	
Saturn	1429	13.51	
Uranus	2875	27 .30	
Neptune	4504	42.61	
Pluto	5900	55.91	

Questions
1. What did you notice about the distances of the inner planets from the Sun compared to the outer planets' distances from the Sun? <u>Answers may vary. For example, the outer planets are much more distant from the Sun.</u>

2. Describe what happened to the distance you traveled around the Sun on each planet's orbit as you got further away from the Sun. <u>Answers may vary. For example, the distance increased greatly.</u>

3. Why do you think it takes a longer period of time for Pluto and Neptune to travel around the Sun than it does for Mercury? <u>The distance from the Sun is so great.</u>

4. If it takes longer for the outer planets to travel around the Sun, what happened to the length of each planet's year? Explain your answer. <u>Answers may vary. For example, the year is much longer.</u>

35   Science Grade 5

page 35

EARTH SCIENCE

Name: _____

Space Snowballs

Planets and moons are not the only objects in our solar system that travel in orbits. Comets also orbit the sun.

A **comet** is like a giant dirty snowball that is $\frac{1}{2}$ to 3 miles wide. It is made of frozen gases, dust, ice and rocks.

As the comet gets closer to the sun, the frozen gases melt and evaporate. Dust particles float in the air. The dust forms a cloud called a **coma**. The "wind" from the sun blows the coma away from the sun. The blowing coma forms the comet's tail.

There are more than 800 known comets. Halley's Comet is the most famous. It appears about every 76 years. The last scheduled appearance in this century was in 1985. When will it appear next?

Find the words from the Word Bank in the word search. When you are finished, write down the letters that are not circled. Start at the top of the puzzle and go from left to right.

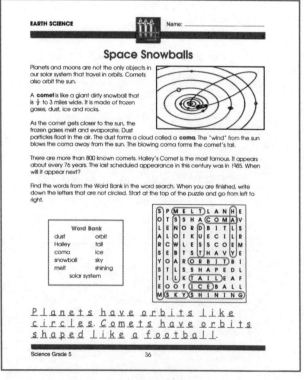

Word Bank	
dust	orbit
Halley	tall
coma	ice
snowball	sky
melt	shining
solar system	

<u>Planets have orbits like circles. Comets have orbits shaped like a football.</u>

Science Grade 5   36

page 36

Science Grade 5   40